Introduction

This is a technical explanation of the Protocol between the United States and Australia, signed on September 27, 2001, (the "Protocol") amending the Convention between the United States of America and Australia for the Avoidance of Double Taxation and the Prevention of Fiscal Evasion with Respect to Taxes on Income, signed on August 6, 1982 (the "Convention").

Negotiations took into account the U.S. Treasury Department's current tax treaty policy, the Treasury Department's Model Income Tax Convention (the "U.S. Model"), published on September 20, 1996, and the Australian Model Tax Convention. Negotiations also took into account the Model Tax Convention on Income and on Capital, published by the Organization for Economic Cooperation and Development, as updated in April 2000 (the "OECD Model"), and recent tax treaties concluded by both countries.

The Technical Explanation is an official guide to the Protocol. It reflects the policies behind particular Protocol provisions, as well as understandings reached with respect to the application and interpretation of the Protocol. References in the Technical Explanation to "he" or "his" should be read to mean "he or she" or "his or her."

Article 1

Article 1 of the Protocol modifies paragraph (3) of Article 1 of the Convention which permits the United States to continue to tax as U.S. citizens former citizens whose loss of citizenship had as one of its principal motives the avoidance of tax. To make the Convention consistent with U.S. law, the Protocol extends this treatment to former long term residents whose loss of such status had as one of its principal purposes the avoidance of tax.

Section 877 of the Internal Revenue Code of 1986 (the "Code") applies to former citizens and long-term residents of the United States whose loss of citizenship or long-term resident status had as one of its principal purposes the avoidance of tax. Under section 877, the United States generally treats an individual as having a principal purpose to avoid tax if either of the following criteria exceed established thresholds: (a) the average annual net income tax of such individual for the period of 5 taxable years ending before the date of the loss of status, or (b) the net worth of such individual as of the date of the loss of status. The thresholds are adjusted annually for inflation. Section 877(c) provides certain exceptions to these presumptions of tax avoidance. The United States defines "long-term resident" as an individual (other than a U.S. citizen) who is a lawful permanent resident of the United States in at least 8 of the prior 15 taxable years. An individual is not treated as a lawful permanent resident for any taxable year if such individual is treated as a resident of a foreign country under the provisions of a tax treaty between the United States and the foreign country and the individual does not waive the benefits of such treaty applicable to residents of the foreign country.

Article 2

Article 2 of the Protocol amends paragraph (1) of Article 2 (Taxes Covered) of the Convention. Article 2 of the Convention specifies the U.S. and Australian taxes to which the Convention applies.

In respect of the United States, the taxes to which the Convention applies currently are the Federal income taxes imposed by the Code, but excluding the accumulated earnings tax and the personal holding company tax. Article 2 of the Protocol amends sub-paragraph (1)(a) of Article 2 (Taxes Covered) of the Convention to provide that all U.S. income taxes are covered taxes for purposes of the Convention. Thus, the accumulated earnings tax and the personal holding company tax are covered taxes because they are income taxes and they are not otherwise excluded from coverage. Under the Code, these taxes will not apply to most foreign corporations because of either a statutory exclusion or the corporation's failure to meet a statutory requirement. The Protocol does not change the Convention's exclusion of social security taxes and excise taxes, such as those imposed on private foundations and foreign insurers, from the taxes covered by the Convention.

In respect of Australia, the tax to which the Convention currently applies is the Australian income tax, including the additional tax upon the undistributed amount of the distributable income of a private company (which has been repealed). Article 2 of the Protocol provides that the covered taxes are (i) the Australian income tax, including tax on capital gains, and (ii) the resource rent tax in respect of offshore projects relating to exploration for or exploitation of petroleum resources ("RRT"), imposed under the federal law of Australia. The specific reference to the Australian capital gains tax makes clear that U.S. taxpayers receive a foreign tax credit for Australian capital gains taxes paid. With respect to the RRT, the Protocol's modifications to the covered Australian taxes mean that the provisions of the Convention, including Article 5 (Permanent Establishment), Article 7 (Business Profits) and Article 27 (Miscellaneous), generally will apply to the RRT. However, the effect of the Protocol's modification to Article 22 (Relief from Double Taxation) is that even though the RRT is a covered tax, the United States is not required by the Convention to grant a U.S. foreign tax credit for RRT paid to Australia. Whether the RRT is creditable therefore is determined under U.S. domestic law.

Article 3

Article 3 of the Protocol amends Article 4 (Residence) of the Convention. Article 4 of the Convention sets forth rules for determining whether a person is a resident of a Contracting State for purposes of the Convention. As a general matter only residents of the Contracting States may claim the benefits of the Convention. The treaty definition of residence is to be used only for purposes of the Convention. The fact that a person is determined to be a resident of a

Contracting State under Article 4 of the Convention does not necessarily entitle that person to the benefits of the Convention. In addition to being a resident, a person also must qualify for benefits under Article 23 (Limitation on Benefits) of the Convention (as amended by the Protocol) in order to receive benefits conferred on residents of a Contracting State.

Sub-paragraph (1)(b) of Article 4 (Residence) of the Convention provides that a person is a resident of the United States for treaty purposes if the person is (i) a United States corporation or (ii) subject to certain exceptions, any other person resident in the United States for United States tax purposes. Paragraph (a) of Article 3 of the Protocol clarifies the treatment of a United States citizen. A United States citizen is treated as a resident of the United States unless the United States citizen is a resident of a State other than Australia for purposes of a double tax agreement between that third State and Australia.

This rule means that a U.S. citizen who is a resident of a country other than the United States or Australia cannot choose the benefits of the Convention over those provided by the tax treaty between Australia and his country of residence. For example, a U.S. citizen who is a resident of the United Kingdom and entitled to full benefits under the U.K.-Australian tax treaty could claim only the benefits of that convention, even if the Convention would provide greater benefits. If a U.S. citizen's country of residence does not have a tax treaty with Australia (or if the U.S. citizen does not qualify as a "resident" of the third State for purposes of the tax treaty between that State and Australia or is otherwise denied benefits of the treaty), then he will be treated as a resident of the United States. If such a person is a resident of both the United States and Australia, whether or not he is to be treated as a resident of the United States for purposes of the Convention is determined by the tie-breaker rules of paragraph (2) of Article 4 of the Convention.

The fact that a U.S. citizen may not be treated as a U.S. resident under the Convention does not alter the application of the saving clause of paragraph (3) of Article 1 (Personal Scope) of the Convention to that citizen. For example, a U.S. citizen who, under this rule, is not considered to be a resident of the United States still is taxable on his worldwide income under the generally applicable rules of the Code.

Article 4

Article 4 of the Protocol adds a new paragraph (9) to Article 7 (Business Profits) of the Convention. Article 7 of the Convention generally provides that business profits of an enterprise of one Contracting State may not be taxed by the other Contracting State unless the enterprise carries on business in that other Contracting State through a permanent establishment (as defined in Article 5 (Permanent Establishment)) situated there. When that condition is met, the State in which the permanent establishment is situated may tax the enterprise on the income that is attributable to the permanent establishment.

The Protocol does not change the basic rules of Article 7 (Business Profits) of the Convention. Rather, new paragraph (9) simply clarifies the treatment of fiscally transparent entities (including trusts) and beneficial owners thereof under Article 7 of the Convention. Australia requested this clarification because, under Australian law, the trustees of a trust, as the legal owner of the trust property, might be regarded as the only person having a permanent establishment (rather than the beneficiaries of the trust, who have a beneficial entitlement to the income but no legal ownership). Thus, absent this clarification, any permanent establishment resulting from that trade or business might be considered to be that of the trustees, rather than that of the beneficiaries.

New paragraph (9) provides that if a fiscally transparent entity (or trustee) has a permanent establishment in a Contracting State and a resident of the other Contracting State is beneficially entitled to a share of the business profits from the business that is carried on by the fiscally transparent entity (or trustee) through that permanent establishment, then the beneficial owner is treated as carrying on a business through a permanent establishment in that Contracting State, and its share of business profits therefrom are attributed to the permanent establishment. Thus, if a trust with a U.S. beneficiary carries on a business in Australia through its trustee, and that trustee's actions rise to the level of a permanent establishment, then the U.S. beneficiary will be treated as having a permanent establishment in Australia and the profits of the trust associated with that permanent establishment will be treated as business profits under Article 7. Since paragraph (9) is added solely to address the Australian law relating to trusts, the absence of similar language in other U.S. tax treaties should not be read as implying that a resident may avoid permanent establishment treatment and business profits by investing through a fiscally transparent entity.

Article 5

Article 5 of the Protocol revises Article 8 (Shipping and Air Transport) of the Convention which governs the taxation of profits from the operation of ships and aircraft in international traffic. Paragraph (1) of Article 8 of the Convention provides that profits derived by a resident of one of the Contracting States from the operation in international traffic of ships or aircraft are taxable only in that Contracting State. In addition to income derived directly from the operation of ships and aircraft in international traffic, this rule also includes certain items of rental income that are closely related to those activities.

Under sub-paragraph (a) of paragraph (1) of Article 8 of the Convention, income of a resident of one of the Contracting States from the rental of ships or aircraft on a full basis (*i.e.*, with crew) operated in international traffic by the lessee is income from the operation of ships and aircraft in international traffic if the resident either operates ships or aircraft in international traffic or regularly leases ships or aircraft on a full basis. Such income is exempt from tax in the other Contracting State. The Protocol does not modify this rule.

Sub-paragraph (b) of paragraph (1) of Article 8 of the Convention currently applies to profits from the lease of ships or aircraft on a bare boat basis (*i.e.*, without crew), or of containers and related equipment, provided that the lease is merely incidental to the operation in international traffic of ships or aircraft by the lessor and the leased ships or aircraft are operated in international traffic, or the containers and related equipment are used in international traffic by the lessee. The Protocol revises this rule to delete the requirement that the leased ships or aircraft actually be operated in international traffic. Thus, paragraph (1) now encompasses income from the lease of ships or aircraft on a bare boat basis when the income is incidental to the operation of ships or aircraft in international traffic by the lessor. Such income is exempt from tax in the other Contracting State. The Protocol makes coverage of bare boat leasing in Article 8 of the Convention generally consistent with Article 8 of the OECD Model, although narrower than in Article 8 of the U.S. Model, which covers income from bare boat leasing without regard to whether it is incidental to the operation of ships or aircraft by the lessor.

The Protocol also deletes the references to containers and related equipment in sub-paragraph (1)(b) of Article 8. Containers (including trailers, barges, and related equipment for the transport of containers) used in international traffic are addressed in new paragraph (2) of Article 8 of the Convention, which tracks the U.S. Model. Under this paragraph, profits of an enterprise of a Contracting State from the use, maintenance or rental of containers (including equipment for their transport) that are used for the transport of goods in international traffic are exempt from tax in the other Contracting State. This result obtains under paragraph (2) regardless of whether the recipient of the income is engaged in the operation of ships or aircraft in international traffic. By contrast, Article 8 of the OECD Model covers only income from the use, maintenance or rental of containers that is incidental to other income from international traffic.

Article 8 of the Convention provides that the rules of the Article apply to income derived though participation in a pool service, in a joint transport operating organization or in an international operating agency. New paragraph (3) of Article 8 of the Convention, as revised by the Protocol, provides that the rules of Article 8 include profits from participation in a pool service or other profit sharing arrangement. This language follows the Australian model tax treaty. It refers to various arrangements for international cooperation by carriers in shipping and air transport. For example, airlines from two countries may agree to share the transport of passengers between the two countries. They each will fly the same number of flights per week and share the revenues from that route equally, regardless of the number of passengers that each airline actually transports. New paragraph (3) makes clear that with respect to each carrier the Article excepts all the income earned by that carrier with respect to the pool service or other profit sharing arrangement, and not just the income derived directly by that carrier.

The Protocol clarifies the rule in Article 8 of the Convention dealing with carriage within a Contracting State as part of international traffic of ships or aircraft. Paragraph (3) of Article 8 of the Convention, prior to amendment by the Protocol, excludes from the definition of operation in international traffic of ships or aircraft profits derived from the carriage of passengers, livestock, mail, goods or merchandise shipped in a Contracting State for discharge at another place in that State. This language has led to questions regarding the treatment of a domestic leg of an international trip. Accordingly, the Protocol clarifies the Article to provide that the carriage of passengers, livestock, mail, goods or merchandise taken on board in a Contracting State for discharge in that State is not operation in international traffic of ships or aircraft and may be taxed in that State. Thus, consistent with the Commentary to Article 8 of the OECD Model, income earned by an enterprise from the inland transport of property or passengers within either Contracting State falls within Article 8 if the transport is undertaken as part of the international transport of property or passengers by the enterprise. Accordingly, if a U.S. shipping company contracts to carry property from Australia to a U.S. city and, as part of that contract, it transports the property by truck from its point of origin to an airport in Australia (or it contracts with a trucking company to carry the property to the airport) the income earned by the U.S. shipping company from the overland leg of the journey would be taxable only in the United States. If a U.S. airline carries passengers from Los Angeles to Perth, with an intervening stop in Melbourne, the Melbourne to Perth leg of the trip would be treated as international transport of passengers with respect to those passengers and would be taxable only in the United States. Similarly, Article 8 would apply to income from lighterage undertaken as part of the international transport of goods.

Article 6

Article 6 of the Protocol replaces Article 10 (Dividends) of the Convention. Article 10 provides rules for the taxation of dividends paid by a company that is a resident of one Contracting State to a beneficial owner that is a resident of the other Contracting State. The Article generally provides for full residence country taxation of such dividends, with a limited source State right to tax. Article 10 also provides rules for the imposition of a tax on branch profits by the State of source. Finally, the Article prohibits a State from imposing taxes on a company resident in the other Contracting State, other than a branch profits tax, on undistributed earnings.

The provisions of this Article apply equally in Australia to both franked and unfranked dividends. Australia has an integrated tax system, under which "franked" dividends (*i.e.*, dividends that are paid out of profits that have already been subject to corporate tax) are not subject to any additional tax at the hands of the shareholder. When the shareholder is a foreign person, franked dividends are exempt from Australian dividend withholding tax by statute. Under Australian law, dividends paid out of untaxed corporate profits, or "unfranked" dividends, are subject to full dividend withholding tax when the shareholder is a foreign person.

Paragraph 1

The right of a shareholder's country of residence to tax dividends arising in the other country is preserved by paragraph (1), which permits a Contracting State to tax its residents on dividends paid to them by a company that is a resident of the other Contracting State. For dividends from any other source (other than for dividends attributable to a permanent establishment in the other State) paid to a resident, Article 21 (Income not Expressly Mentioned) grants the residence country exclusive taxing jurisdiction.

Paragraph 2

The State of source also may tax dividends to which a resident of the other State is beneficially entitled, subject to the limitations of paragraphs (2) and (3). Paragraph (2) generally limits the withholding tax in the State of source to 15 percent of the gross amount of the dividend. If, however, the beneficial owner of the dividend is a company resident in the other State and owns directly shares representing at least 10 percent of the voting power of the company paying the dividend, then the withholding tax in the State of source is limited to 5 percent of the gross amount of the dividend. Shares are considered voting shares if they provide the power to elect, appoint or replace any person vested with the powers ordinarily exercised by the board of directors of a U.S. corporation.

The benefits of paragraph (2) may be granted at the time of payment by means of reduced withholding at source. It also is consistent with the paragraph for tax to be withheld at the time of payment at full statutory rates, and the treaty benefit to be granted by means of a subsequent refund, so long as such procedures are applied in a reasonable manner.

Paragraph (2) does not affect the taxation of the profits out of which the dividends are paid. The taxation by a Contracting State of the income of its resident companies is governed by the internal law of the Contracting State, subject to the provisions of Article 23 (Non-Discrimination).

The term "beneficially entitled" is not defined in the Convention, and is, therefore, defined as under the internal law of the country imposing tax (*i.e.*, the source State). A person "beneficially entitled" to a dividend is the "beneficial owner" of the dividend. Thus, the resident beneficially entitled to a dividend for purposes of Article 10 is the person to which the dividend income is attributable for tax purposes under the laws of the source State. Therefore, if a dividend paid by a corporation that is a resident of one of the States (as determined under Article 4 (Residence)) is received by a nominee or agent that is a resident of the other State on behalf of a person that is not a resident of that other State, the dividend is not entitled to the benefits of this Article. However, a dividend received by a nominee on behalf of a resident of that other State would be entitled to benefits. These limitations are confirmed by paragraph 12 of the OECD Commentary to Article 10. See also paragraph 24 of the Commentary to Article 1 of the OECD Model.

Companies holding shares through fiscally transparent entities such as partnerships are considered for purposes of this paragraph to hold their proportionate interest in the shares held by the intermediate entity. As a result, companies holding shares through such entities may be able to claim the benefits of sub-paragraph (a) under certain circumstances. The lower rate of withholding tax applies when the company's proportionate share of the shares held by the intermediate entity meets the 10 percent threshold. Whether this ownership threshold is satisfied may be difficult to determine and often will require an analysis of the partnership or trust agreement.

If either country modifies significantly its law regarding taxation of corporations or dividends, then the United States and Australia agree to consult with each other to determine any appropriate amendment to paragraph (2).

Paragraph 3

As described below, paragraph (3) provides for exclusive residence country taxation of dividends (i.e., a zero rate of withholding tax) with respect to certain dividends distributed by a company resident in one Contracting State to a company resident in the other Contracting State.

Paragraph (3) reduces the rate of withholding tax to zero on dividends beneficially owned by a company that has owned directly at least 80 percent of the voting power of the company paying the dividend for the 12-month period ending on the date the dividend is declared. To be eligible for the rule in this paragraph, the 80 percent owner must meet the public trading requirements of paragraph (2)(c) of Article 16 (Limitation on Benefits), as revised by the Protocol, or be granted such benefit by the competent authorities pursuant to paragraph (5) of Article 16, as revised by the Protocol.

These restrictions are necessary because of the increased pressure on the Limitation on Benefits tests resulting from the fact that the Convention is one of the few U.S. tax treaties to provide for a zero rate of withholding tax on intercompany dividends. The tests are intended to prevent companies from reorganizing in order to become eligible for the zero rate of withholding tax in circumstances where the Limitation on Benefits provision alone may not provide sufficient protection against treaty-shopping.

For example, assume that ThirdCo is a company resident in a third State. ThirdCo owns directly 100% of the issued and outstanding voting stock of USCo, a U.S. company, and of AusCo, an Australian company. AusCo is a substantial company that brews beer; USCo distributes that beer in the United States. If ThirdCo contributes to AusCo all the stock of USCo, dividends paid by USCo to AusCo would satisfy the active trade or business test of paragraph (3) of Article 16. However, allowing ThirdCo to qualify for the zero rate of withholding tax, which is not available to it under the third State's tax treaty (if any) with the United States, would encourage treaty-shopping.

In order to prevent this type of treaty-shopping, the Protocol requires the company receiving the dividends to meet the publicly traded requirements of paragraph (2)(c) of Article 16 (or, as described below, to be granted such benefit by the competent authorities pursuant to paragraph (5) of Article 16). It is not sufficient for the company to qualify for treaty benefits generally under the "active conduct of a trade or business" test (paragraph 3 of Article 16), the "ownership-base erosion" test (paragraph 2(g) of Article 16), or the "headquarters company" test (paragraph 2(h) of Article 16).

If a company does not qualify for the zero rate of withholding tax under the publicly traded test, it may request a determination from the relevant competent authority pursuant to paragraph 5 of Article 16 (Limitation on Benefits) of the Convention, as revised by the Protocol. Benefits will be granted with respect to a dividend if the competent authority of the Contracting State in which the income arises determines that the establishment, acquisition or maintenance of such resident and the conduct of its operations did not have as one of its principal purposes the obtaining of benefits under the Convention.

Paragraph 4

Sub-paragraphs (a) through (c) provide rules for the treatment of dividends paid by a Regulated Investment Company (RIC) or a Real Estate Investment Trust (REIT) that are consistent with U.S. treaty policy.

Sub-paragraph (a) provides that dividends paid by a RIC or REIT are not eligible for the 5 percent maximum rate of withholding tax of sub-paragraph (a) of paragraph 2 or the 0 percent rate of withholding tax of paragraph (3).

Sub-paragraph (b) provides that the 15 percent maximum rate of sub-paragraph (2)(b) applies to dividends paid by RICs.

Sub-paragraph (c) provides that the 15 percent maximum rate of withholding tax applies to dividends paid by a REIT, provided that one of three conditions is met. First, the dividend may qualify for the 15 percent maximum rate if the person beneficially entitled to the dividend is an individual holding an interest of not more than 10 percent in the REIT. Second, the dividend may qualify for the 15 percent maximum rate if it is paid with respect to a class of stock that is publicly traded and the person beneficially entitled to the dividend is a person holding an interest of not more than 5 percent of any class of the REIT's stock. Third, the dividend may qualify for the 15 percent maximum rate if the person beneficially entitled to the dividend holds an interest in the REIT of 10 percent or less and the REIT is "diversified" (*i.e.*, the gross value of no single interest in real property held by the REIT exceeds 10 percent of the gross value of the REIT's total interest in real property). For purposes of this diversification test, foreclosure property is not considered an interest in real property, and a REIT holding a partnership interest is treated as owning its proportionate share of any interest in real property held by the partnership.

The restrictions set out above are intended to prevent the use of these entities to gain inappropriate U.S. tax benefits for certain shareholders resident in Australia. For example, a company resident in Australia that wishes to hold a diversified portfolio of U.S. corporate shares could hold the portfolio directly and pay a U.S. withholding tax of 15 percent on all of the dividends that it receives. Alternatively, it could hold the same diversified portfolio by purchasing 10 percent or more of the interests in a RIC. If the RIC is a pure conduit, there may be no U.S. tax cost to interposing the RIC in the chain of ownership. Absent the special rule in paragraph (4), such use of the RIC could transform portfolio dividends, taxable in the United States under the Convention at a 15 percent maximum rate of withholding tax, into direct investment dividends taxable at a zero or 5 percent maximum rate of withholding tax.

Similarly, a resident of Australia directly holding U.S. real property would pay U.S. tax either at a 30 percent rate of withholding tax on the gross income or at graduated rates on the net income. As in the preceding example, by placing the real property in a REIT, the investor could transform real estate income into dividend income, taxable at the rates provided in Article 10, significantly reducing the U.S. tax that otherwise would be imposed. Paragraph (4) prevents this result and thereby avoids a disparity between the taxation of direct real estate investments and real estate investments made through REIT conduits. In the cases covered by the exceptions, the holding in the REIT is not considered the equivalent of a direct holding in the underlying real property.

Special rules apply to REIT dividends paid to an Australian unit trust registered as a "Management Investment Scheme" under the Australian Corporations Act in which the principal class of units is listed on a recognized stock exchange in Australia and regularly traded on one or more recognized stock exchanges (a listed Australian property trust or "LAPT"). These special rules apply because LAPTs receive tax benefits under Australian law that are similar to those received by REITs in the United States, in order to encourage collective investment by small unitholders. The tax benefits are intended to replicate the tax treatment of direct investment by these unitholders. Therefore, this Australian policy was accommodated by granting small unitholders of LAPTs the same benefits with respect to REIT shares held by the LAPT that they would get if they held the REIT shares directly.

Sub-paragraph (d) first provides that the provisions of paragraph (2)(b) shall apply with respect to dividends paid by a REIT to an LAPT, notwithstanding sub-paragraph (c). Recognizing the importance of maintaining the anti-abuse character of the rule, however, sub-paragraph (d) further provides that the 15 percent maximum rate of withholding tax does not automatically apply to all the dividends paid by a REIT to an LAPT with large unitholders. If a unitholder owns 5 percent or more of the beneficial interests in an LAPT and the responsible entity for the LAPT knows or has reason to know of such ownership, then the unitholder is subject to a look-through rule. Each 5 percent owner is deemed to hold directly his proportionate interest in the REIT held through the LAPT and the unitholder must meet the tests of sub-paragraph (c) (taking into account all shares owned by the unitholder in the REIT whether directly or through application of the look-through rule to one or more LAPTs) if he is to qualify for the 15 percent maximum rate of withholding tax.

In applying these tests, the REIT shares with respect to which the dividends have been paid are deemed to be publicly traded. However, an LAPT, in order to receive the beneficial treatment of sub-paragraph (d), must have its principal class of units listed on a recognized stock exchange in Australia and regularly traded on one or more recognized stock exchanges as defined in Article 16 (Limitation on Benefits) as modified by the Protocol.

As an example, assume that an LAPT owns 40 percent of a REIT. One LAPT unitholder, an individual named A, owns 20 percent of the beneficial interests in the LAPT, and the responsible entity for the LAPT knows of the percentage of A's ownership interests. Each other LAPT unitholder holds less than 5 percent of the beneficial interests in the LAPT. The LAPT's principal class of units is listed and regularly traded on a recognized exchange in Australia. In addition to his interest in the LAPT, A owns directly 5 percent of the beneficial interests in the REIT.

Because A owns at least 5 percent of the LAPT and the responsible entity for the LAPT knows of this fact, A is treated as holding a portion of the LAPT's direct interest in the REIT equal to his proportionate interest in the LAPT. Thus, A is treated as owning 8 percent of the REIT (.40 X .20) through his LAPT investment. Because A's beneficial interests in the REIT total 13 percent (8 percent held through the LAPT plus 5 percent held directly), sub-paragraph (c) denies A the benefits of the 15 percent maximum rate of withholding tax with respect to dividends paid by the REIT. The LAPT is, however, eligible for the 15 percent maximum rate on the remaining 80 percent of the dividends paid by the REIT to the LAPT (the proportion of the REIT shares that are not attributable to A's ownership interest).

Paragraph 5

Paragraph (5) excludes from the general source country limitations under paragraphs (2) and (3) dividends paid with respect to holdings that form part of the business property of a permanent establishment or fixed base situated in the source country. Such dividends will be taxed on a net basis using the rates and rules of taxation generally applicable to residents of the State in which the permanent establishment or fixed base is located, as modified by the Convention. An example of dividends paid with respect to the business property of a permanent establishment or fixed base would be dividends derived by a dealer in stock or securities from stock or securities that the dealer held for sale to customers. In such case, Article 7 applies with respect to business profits from a permanent establishment and Article 14 applies to income from the performance of personal services in an independent capacity from a fixed base.

Paragraph 6

Paragraph (6) defines the term "dividends" broadly and flexibly. The definition is intended to cover all arrangements that yield a return on an equity investment in a corporation as determined under the tax law of the State of source, as well as arrangements that might be developed in the future.

The term dividends includes income from shares, or other corporate rights that are not treated as debt under the law of the source State, that participate in the profits of the company. The term also includes income that is subjected to the same tax treatment as income from shares by the law of the source State. Thus, a constructive dividend that results from a non-arm's length transaction between a corporation and a related party is a dividend. Similarly, a payment denominated as interest that is made by a thinly capitalized corporation may be treated as a dividend to the extent that the debt is recharacterized as equity under the laws of the source State.

In the case of the United States, the term dividends includes amounts treated as a dividend under U.S. law upon the sale or redemption of shares or upon a transfer of shares in a reorganization. See, *e.g.*, Rev. Rul. 92-85, 1992-2 C.B. 69 (sale of foreign subsidiary's stock to U.S. sister company is a deemed dividend to extent of subsidiary's and sister's earnings and profits). Further, a distribution from a U.S. publicly traded partnership, which is taxed as a corporation under U.S. law, is a dividend for purposes of Article 10. However, a distribution by a limited liability company is not characterized by the United States as a dividend and, therefore, is not a dividend for purposes of Article 10, provided the limited liability company is not taxable as a corporation under U.S. law.

Paragraph 7

A State's right to tax dividends paid by a company that is a resident of the other State is restricted by paragraph (7) to cases in which the dividends are paid to a resident of the first State, or are attributable to a permanent establishment or fixed base situated in that State. Thus, a State may not impose a "secondary" withholding tax on dividends paid by a nonresident company out of earnings and profits from that State. In the case of the United States, paragraph (7) overrides the ability to impose taxes under sections 871 and 882(a) on dividends paid by foreign corporations that have a U.S. source under section 861(a)(2)(B). The Convention currently allows the imposition of each of these taxes.

The paragraph also restricts a State's right to impose corporate level taxes on undistributed profits, other than a branch profits tax. The accumulated earnings tax and the personal holding company taxes are taxes covered in Article 2 (Taxes Covered). Accordingly, under the provisions of Article 7 (Business Profits), the United States may not impose those taxes on the income of a resident of the other State except to the extent that income is attributable to a permanent establishment in the United States. Paragraph (7) further confirms the restriction on the U.S. authority to impose those taxes. The paragraph does not restrict a State's right to tax its resident shareholders on undistributed earnings of a corporation resident in the other State. Thus, the U.S. authority to impose the foreign personal holding company tax, the taxes on subpart F income and on an increase in earnings invested in U.S. property, and the tax on income of a passive foreign investment company that is a qualified electing fund is in no way restricted by this provision.

Paragraph 8

Paragraph (8) permits a State to impose a branch profits tax on a company resident in the other State. The tax is in addition to other taxes permitted by the Convention. The term "company" is defined in Article 3 (General Definitions) of the Convention.

A State may impose a branch profits tax on a corporation if the corporation has income attributable to a permanent establishment in that State, derives income from real property in that State that is taxed on a net basis under Article 6 (Income from Real Property), or realizes gains taxable in that State under paragraph (1) or (3) of Article 13 (Alienation of Property). The tax is limited, however, to the aforementioned items of income that are included in the "dividend equivalent amount."

The term "dividend equivalent amount" for any year approximates the dividend that a U.S. branch office would have paid during the year if the branch had been operated as a separate U.S. subsidiary company. Generally, the dividend equivalent amount for a particular year is the income described above that is included in the corporation's effectively connected earnings and profits for that year, after payment of the corporate tax under Articles 6 (Income from Real Property), 7 (Business Profits), or 13 (Alienation of Property), reduced for any increase in the branch's U.S. net equity during the year or increased for any reduction in its U.S. net equity during the year. U.S. net equity is U.S. assets less U.S. liabilities. See Treas. Reg. section 1.884-1. The United States may not impose its branch profits tax on the business profits of a corporation resident in Australia that are effectively connected with a U.S. trade or business but that are not attributable to a permanent establishment and are not otherwise subject to U.S. taxation under Article 6 (Income from Real Property) or paragraph (1) or (3) of Article 13 (Alienation of Property).

Australia currently does not impose a branch profits tax. If Australia were to impose such a tax, the base of such a tax would be limited to an amount analogous to the U.S. dividend equivalent amount.

The branch profits tax will not be imposed, however, if certain requirements are met. In general, these requirements provide rules for a branch that parallel the rules for when a dividend paid by a subsidiary will be subject to exclusive residence country taxation. Accordingly, the branch profits tax may not be imposed in the case of a company which is a qualified person by reason of sub-paragraph (c) of paragraph (2) or paragraph (5) of Article 16 (Limitation on Benefits) (*i.e.*, a publicly-traded company, a subsidiary of a publicly-traded company or a company granted treaty benefits by the competent authorities).

Moreover, the transfer of assets from a branch that meets the requirements for an exemption under paragraph 8 into a subsidiary that meets the requirements of paragraph 3 should not change this result. Accordingly, in that case, it is expected that the U.S. competent authority will exercise its discretion to treat the new parent-subsidiary group as qualified for the zero rate of withholding tax as well, so long as the Australian parent meets the 80-percent ownership requirement of paragraph 3 with respect to the subsidiary.

Paragraph 9

Paragraph (9) provides that the branch profits tax permitted by paragraph (8) shall not be imposed at a rate of withholding tax exceeding the maximum direct investment dividend rate of withholding tax of 5 percent. This rule will apply only if the conditions related to the exemption described above in paragraph (8) are not met.

Relation to Other Articles

Notwithstanding the foregoing limitations on source State taxation of dividends, the saving clause of paragraph (3) of Article 1 (Personal Scope) permits the United States to tax dividends received by its residents and citizens, subject to the special foreign tax credit rules of paragraph (4) of Article 22 (Relief from Double Taxation), as if the Convention had not come into effect.

The benefits of this Article are also subject to the provisions of Article 16 (Limitation on Benefits). Thus, if a resident of Australia is beneficially entitled to dividends paid by a U.S. company, the shareholder must qualify for treaty benefits under at least one of the tests of Article 16 in order to receive the benefits of this Article.

While the provisions of this Article will enter into force with the rest of the Protocol, Article 13 of the Protocol provides that dividends paid by a REIT to an LAPT will not be subject to Article 10 (Dividends) as amended by the Protocol if, generally, the REIT shares in respect of which the dividends were paid were owned by the LAPT on or before March 26, 2001 (the date on which negotiation of the Protocol began).

Article 7

Article 7 of the Protocol replaces Article 11 (Interest) of the Convention. Article 11 provides rules for the taxation of interest arising in one Contracting State and paid to a beneficial owner that is a resident of the other Contracting State.

Paragraph 1

Paragraph (1) generally grants to the State of residence the non-exclusive right to tax interest to which its residents are beneficially entitled and which arises in the other Contracting State. Paragraph (1) is similar to existing paragraph (1) of Article 11 of the Convention.

The term "beneficially entitled" is not defined in the Convention, and is, therefore, defined under the internal law of the State of source. The person beneficially entitled to interest for purposes of Article 11 is the beneficial owner of the interest, *i.e.*, the person to which the interest income is attributable for tax purposes under the laws of the State of source. Thus, if interest arising in a Contracting State is received by a nominee or agent that is a resident of the other State on behalf of a person that is not a resident of that other State, the interest is not entitled to the benefits of Article 11. However, interest received by a nominee on behalf of a resident of that other State would be entitled to benefits. These limitations are confirmed by paragraph 8 of the OECD Commentary to Article 11. See also paragraph 24 of the OECD Commentary to Article 1.

Paragraph 2

Paragraph (2) is similar to existing paragraph (2) of Article 11 of the Convention. It provides that the State of source also may tax interest to which a resident of the other State is beneficially entitled, subject to a maximum rate of 10 percent.

Paragraph 3

Paragraph (3) provides for exclusive residence based taxation in certain cases.

Under sub-paragraph (a), interest received by a Contracting State or a political or administrative subdivision or a local authority of the Contracting State (i.e., in the United States a State or local government) is subject to exclusive residence based taxation. This rule also applies to any other body exercising governmental functions in one of the two States or a bank performing central banking functions in one of the two States.

Sub-paragraph (b) provides that interest received by a financial institution is subject to exclusive residence based taxation if the financial institution is unrelated to the payer. A financial institution is unrelated to the payer of the interest if the financial institution and payer are not treated as Associated Enterprises under Article 9 (Associated Enterprises) of the Convention, and the financial institution and payer otherwise deal with each other in an arm's-length manner. For this purpose, a financial institution is a bank or other entity that issues debt or takes deposits and uses those funds to carry on a business of providing finance. Thus, a financial institution regulated as a bank under the Federal Depository Institutions Act would be a financial institution, as would an entity that issues debt in financial markets and uses that debt, directly or indirectly, to lend money or purchase debt obligations. Investment banks, brokers and commercial finance companies (but not captive financing companies) are covered by this exemption provided that they obtain their funds by borrowing from the public.

Paragraph 4

Sub-paragraph (a) of paragraph (4) contains an exception to paragraph (3)(b). This exception permits source State taxation (at the 10 percent maximum rate applicable to interest generally under the Article) if the interest is paid as part of an arrangement involving back-to-back loans or their economic equivalent.

By referencing the economic equivalent of a back-to-back loan, paragraph (4)(a) reaches transactions that would not meet the legal requirements of a loan, but would nevertheless serve that purpose economically. For example, the term would encompass securities issued at a discount, or certain swap arrangements intended to operate as the economic equivalent of a back-to-back loan.

Sub-paragraph (b) of paragraph (4) preserves the application of the domestic tax law of each State regarding anti-avoidance provisions. Thus, nothing in Article 11 limits the ability of the United States to enforce existing anti-avoidance provisions, regardless of whether those provisions are targeted (*e.g.*, regulation section 1.881-3 and regulations adopted under the authority of section 7701(l) of the Code) or of broad application (*e.g.*, Code section 267). The provision also does not limit the ability of a country to adopt new anti-abuse provisions.

Paragraph 5

Paragraph 5 defines the term "interest" broadly and flexibly. Interest that is paid or accrued subject to a contingency is within the ambit of Article 11. This includes income from a debt obligation carrying the right to participate in profits. The term does not, however, include amounts that are treated as dividends under Article 10 (Dividends). Penalty charges for late payment are excluded from the definition of interest.

The term interest also includes amounts subject to the same tax treatment as income from money lent under the law of the State in which the income arises. Thus, for purposes of the Convention, amounts that the United States will treat as interest include (i) the difference between the issue price and the stated redemption price at maturity of a debt instrument (*i.e.*, original issue discount ("OID")), which may be wholly or partially realized on the disposition of a debt instrument (section 1273), (ii) amounts that are imputed interest on a deferred sales contract (section 483), (iii) amounts treated as interest or OID under the stripped bond rules (section 1286), (iv) amounts treated as OID under the below-market interest rate rules (section 7872), (v) a partner's distributive share of a partnership's interest income (section 702), (vi) the interest portion of periodic payments made under a "finance lease" or similar contractual arrangement that in substance is a borrowing by the nominal lessee to finance the acquisition of property, (vii) amounts included in the income of a holder of a residual interest in a REMIC (section 860E), and (viii) interest with respect to notional principal contracts that are recharacterized as loans because of a "substantial non-periodic payment".

Paragraph 6

Paragraph (6) provides an exception to paragraphs (1), (2), (3) and (4) where the person beneficially entitled to the interest carries on business through a permanent establishment (or performs independent services from a fixed base) in the State of source and the interest is attributable to that permanent establishment (or fixed base). In such cases, the applicable provisions of Article 7 (Business Profits) or Article 14 (Independent Personal Services) will apply.

Paragraph 7

Paragraph (7) provides a source rule that is identical in substance to the interest source rule of the OECD Model. Interest is considered to arise in a Contracting State if paid by a resident of that State. As an exception, interest that is borne by a permanent establishment or fixed base in one of the States is considered to arise in that State. For this purpose, interest is considered to be borne by a permanent establishment or fixed base if it is allocable to taxable income of that permanent establishment or fixed base. If the actual amount of interest on the books of a U.S. branch of a company resident in Australia exceeds the amount of interest allocated to the branch under Treas. Reg. Section 1.882-5, the amount of such excess will not be considered U.S. source interest for purposes of this Article.

Paragraph 8

Paragraph (8) provides that, in cases involving special relationships between persons, Article 11 applies only to that portion of the total interest payments between those persons that would have been made absent such special relationships (*i.e.*, an arm's-length interest payment). Any excess amount of interest paid remains taxable according to the laws of the United States and Australia, respectively, with due regard to the other provisions of the Convention. Thus, if the excess amount would be treated under the source State's law as a distribution of profits by a corporation, such amount would be taxed as a dividend rather than as interest, but the tax would be subject, if appropriate, to the rate limitations of Article 10 (Dividends).

The term "special relationship" is not defined in the Convention. In applying this paragraph, the United States considers the term to include the relationships described in Article 9 (Associated Enterprises), which in turn correspond to the definition of "control" for purposes of section 482 of the Code.

This paragraph does not address cases where, owing to a special relationship between the payer and the beneficial owner, or between both of them and some other person, the amount of the interest is less than an arm's-length amount. In those cases a transaction may be characterized to reflect its substance and interest may be imputed consistent with the definition of interest in paragraph (2). Consistent with Article 9 (Associated Enterprises), the United States would apply section 482 or 7872 of the Code to determine the amount of imputed interest in those cases.

Paragraph 9

Paragraph (9) provides two anti-abuse exceptions to paragraphs (1), (2), (3) and (4).

Sub-paragraph (a) applies to so-called "contingent interest." Under sub-paragraph (a) of paragraph 9, interest that is paid by a resident of one of the Contracting States to a resident of the other Contracting State that is determined by reference to the profits of the debtor or a related person may be taxed in the Contracting State in which it arises, and according to the laws of that State. The gross amount of the interest may be taxed at a rate not exceeding 15 percent (the rate prescribed in sub-paragraph (b) of paragraph 2 of Article 10 (Dividends)).

Sub-paragraph (b) provides an anti-abuse exception to paragraphs 1 through 4 for excess inclusions from vehicles used to securitize real estate mortgages or other assets. Sub-paragraph (b) serves as a backstop to Code section 860G(b). That section generally requires that a foreign person holding a residual interest in a real estate mortgage investment conduit ("REMIC") take into account for U.S. tax purposes "any excess inclusion" and "amounts includible…[under the REMIC provisions] when paid or distributed (or when the interest is disposed of)…."

Without a full tax at source, non-U.S. transferees of residual interests would have a competitive advantage over U.S. transferees at the time these interests are initially offered. Absent this rule, the United States would suffer a revenue loss with respect to mortgages held in a REMIC because of opportunities for tax avoidance created by differences in the timing of taxable and economic income produced by such interests. In many cases, the transfer to the foreign person is simply disregarded under Reg. § 1.860G-3. Sub-paragraph (b) also serves to indicate that excess inclusions from REMICs are not considered "other income" subject to Article 21 (Income Not Expressly Mentioned) of the Convention.

Sub-paragraph (b) is analogous to subparagraph (b) of paragraph 5 of the U.S. Model, except that it is drafted to apply bilaterally and it applies to securitization of non-real estate assets as well. Thus, for U.S. tax purposes, the withholding tax imposed "to the extent that the amount of interest paid exceeds the normal rate of return on publicly-traded debt instruments with a similar risk profile" is the withholding tax that would be imposed upon an excess inclusion with respect to a residual interest in a REMIC.

Paragraph 10

Paragraph 10 extends the coverage of the Article to include excess interest payments, as defined by Code section 884(f), deemed to be received by a corporation resident in the other Contracting State, which are allocated as interest expense for purposes of determining income attributable to its U.S. permanent establishment or taxable on a net basis in the United States as income from real property or gain on real property to the extent such deductible amounts exceed the interest paid by the permanent establishment or trade or business.

Relation to Other Articles

Notwithstanding the foregoing limitations on source country taxation of interest, the saving clause of paragraph (3) of Article 1 (General Scope) permits the United States to tax its residents and citizens, subject to the special foreign tax credit rules of paragraph (4) of Article 22 (Relief from Double Taxation), as if the Convention had not come into force.

The benefits of this Article are also subject to the provisions of Article 16 (Limitation on Benefits). Thus, if a resident of Australia is beneficially entitled to interest paid by a U.S. corporation, the resident must qualify for treaty benefits under at least one of the tests of Article 16 in order to receive the benefits of this Article.

Article 8

Article 8 of the Protocol amends Article 12 (Royalties) of the Convention.

Paragraph (a) of Article 8 of the Protocol reduces the maximum rate of withholding tax in paragraph (2) of Article 12 of the Convention to 5 percent from 10 percent.

Paragraph (b) of Article 8 of the Protocol replaces sub-paragraph (a) of paragraph (4) of Article 12 of the Convention, which defines "royalties" for purposes of Article 12. The new provision narrows the definition in two ways. First, the Protocol eliminates the portion of the old definition relating to payments for the use of "industrial, commercial or scientific equipment, other than equipment let under a hire purchase agreement." Thus, payments for the use of or the right to use any industrial, commercial or scientific equipment are treated as business profits and are therefore taxable by the source State only if the recipient of the payments has a permanent establishment situated in the source State. Second, to reflect technological advances since the Convention was signed the definition of royalties is extended to cover films and audio and video tapes and disks as well as any other means of image or sound reproduction or transmission, pursuant to television, radio, or other broadcasting. Thus, the new definition would apply to a payment by an Australian broadcaster to a U.S. company for the right to transmit a live feed of an entertainment program over the airwaves or through cable, satellite or the Internet. It would not, however, apply to payments made by a retail customer who has subscribed to satellite television service provided by a U.S. company.

Article 9

Article 9 of the Protocol revises Article 13 (Alienation of Property) of the Convention by replacing paragraph (3) and adding three additional paragraphs.

New paragraph (3) of Article 13, as revised by the Protocol, deals with the taxation of certain gains from the alienation of property, other than real property, forming part of the business property of a permanent establishment that an enterprise of a Contracting State has in the other Contracting State or that pertains to a fixed base available to a resident of a Contracting State situated in the other State for the purpose of performing independent personal services. This also includes gains from the alienation of such permanent establishment (alone or with the whole enterprise) or fixed base. Such gains may be taxed in the State in which the permanent establishment or fixed base is located.

A resident of Australia that is a partner in a partnership doing business in the United States will have a permanent establishment in the United States as a result of the activities of the partnership, assuming that the activities of the partnership rise to the level of a permanent establishment. Rev. Rul. 91-32,1991-1 CB 107. Further, under paragraph (3) of Article 13, as revised by the Protocol, the United States generally may tax a partner's distributive share of income realized by a partnership on the disposition of personal (movable) property forming part of the business property of the partnership in the United States. This result is confirmed by the addition of paragraph (9) of Article 7 (Business Profits).

Paragraph (4) of Article 13, as added by the Protocol, limits the taxing jurisdiction of the State of source with respect to gains from the alienation of ships, aircraft or containers operated or used in international traffic, and from property (other than real property) pertaining to the operation or use of such ships, aircraft, or containers.

Under paragraph (4), such income is taxable only in the Contracting State in which the seller is resident. Notwithstanding paragraph (3), the rules of this paragraph apply even if the income is attributable to a permanent establishment maintained by the enterprise in the other Contracting State.

Paragraph (5) addresses the situation in which a resident of one State emigrates to the other State and, as a result, is subject to special tax rules. Under current law this paragraph would apply only to an Australian resident who expatriates to the United States.

Under Australian domestic tax law, an individual surrendering Australian residence is generally treated as recognizing gain as though he disposed of all assets that do not have the necessary connection with Australia immediately prior to surrendering Australian residence. Assets that have the necessary connection with Australia are not subject to tax under this deemed sale rule because the individual will be subject to Australian tax on the actual sale or disposition of those assets, *i.e.*, the assets are subject to Australian tax jurisdiction regardless of the owner's residence. Assets that have the necessary connection to Australia include interests in an Australian private company or trust, Australian real property, property used in the conduct of a business in Australia through a permanent establishment, and holdings of 10 percent or more in Australian public companies and unit trusts.

Paragraph (5) permits an individual who changes residence from Australia to the United States to elect to be treated for U.S. tax purposes as if he had, immediately before ceasing to be a resident of Australia, sold property and reacquired it for an amount equal to its fair market value. This paragraph has two significant consequences. First, the "deemed sale" rule will result in the individual (still a resident of Australia) triggering gain on assets that the United States is permitted to tax as the source State (*e.g.*, a U.S. real property interest or property part of a permanent establishment). If the individual is subject to U.S. tax on the gain from the deemed sale of the asset, he will be eligible for a foreign tax credit against Australian income tax on the deemed sale (with such resourcing of the gain as is necessary for Australia to provide relief pursuant to Article 22 of the Convention). Second, the "deemed sale and repurchase" will result in the individual (now a U.S. resident) having a "stepped up" basis equal to fair market value in all assets subject to the deemed sale and repurchase, regardless of whether any U.S. tax was triggered by the deemed sale.

Paragraph (6) addresses the situation in which an individual who is a resident of one State expatriates to the other State but elects to defer all or a portion of the tax otherwise due upon expatriation. As with paragraph (5), under current law this paragraph would apply only to an Australian resident who expatriates to the United States.

Although Australian domestic tax law generally requires an individual losing Australian residence to recognize all unrealized gain on assets that do not have the necessary connection with Australia, it permits the individual to defer all or a portion of the gain by electing to treat assets that otherwise lack the necessary connection with Australia as having such necessary connection. As a result of this election, the asset becomes subject to Australian taxing jurisdiction regardless of its location or relationship to Australia, and the former Australian resident will be subject to Australian tax on its actual sale. Under paragraph (6), if an individual changes residence from Australia to the United States and makes this election under Australian domestic law, then only the United States may tax the individual on gain from the assets subject to the election.

The following example illustrates the operation of both paragraphs (5) and (6). An individual emigrates from Australia to the United States. Prior to emigration, the individual has four assets: Australian real property with a basis of $100 and a fair market value of $500, stock in a U.S. company with a basis of $50 and a fair market value of $75, U.S. real property with a basis of $200 and a fair market value of $300, and stock in a New Zealand company with a basis of $200 and a fair market value of $250. Under Australian domestic law, only the Australian real property has the necessary connection with Australia. Because Australia retains taxing jurisdiction over the Australian property, the Australian property is not covered by paragraph (5) or (6) of this Article.

Unless the individual makes an election under Australian law to treat the U.S. stock, the U.S. real property, and the New Zealand stock as having an Australian connection, the taxpayer upon emigration would be subject to Australian tax on the $25 in unrealized gain on the U.S. stock, the $100 in unrealized gain on the U.S. real property, and the $50 in unrealized gain on the New Zealand stock. Under paragraph (5), the individual may elect to be treated for U.S. tax purposes as if he sold and repurchased the U.S. stock, the U.S. real property, and the New Zealand stock. The United States would tax the $100 in gain on the deemed sale of the U.S. real property pursuant to paragraph (1) of Article 13 of the Convention and section 871 of the Internal Revenue Code. In contrast, the individual would most likely not owe any U.S. tax on the gain of either the U.S. or New Zealand stock. If the individual did incur U.S. tax on the deemed sale of the stock (*e.g.*, because either or both the U.S. and New Zealand stock forms part of the business property of a permanent establishment in the United States), then the individual would owe U.S. tax on the deemed sale of the stock, but he would be able to credit all or a portion of that U.S. tax against his Australian tax arising from the deemed sale of the stock. Accordingly, upon emigrating, the individual would be treated, for U.S. tax purposes, as having a basis in the U.S. real property of $300, a basis in the U.S. stock of $75, and a basis in the New Zealand stock of $250. The individual's basis in the Australian real property would remain $100 because no gain was triggered pursuant to the emigration.

If the individual elects to treat the U.S. and New Zealand stock as having a connection with Australia, then the individual will not owe Australian tax on the deemed sale of the two assets. If the individual sells the U.S. or New Zealand stock while a resident of the United States, he will not be taxable in Australia on the gain. If the individual sells the Australian real property while a resident of the United States, he will, however, be taxable by Australia on the gain from the sale of the Australian real property (pursuant to paragraph (1) of Article 13 of the Convention). Under Article 27 (Miscellaneous) of the Convention, any income that is derived by a resident of the United States that may be taxed by Australia pursuant to the Convention is resourced as necessary to permit relief from double taxation under Article 22 (Relief from Double Taxation) of the Convention.

Paragraph 7

Paragraph (7) provides a residual rule for the taxation of capital gains not mentioned in this Article. It states that, except for the special rules set forth in the prior paragraphs, each State may tax capital gains in the manner provided by its domestic law. Under Article 27 (Miscellaneous) of the Convention, any income that is derived by a resident of the United States or Australia that may be taxed by the other State pursuant to the Convention is resourced as necessary to permit relief from double taxation under Article 22 (Relief from Double Taxation) of the Convention.

Article 10

Article 10 of the Protocol replaces Article 16 (Limitation on Benefits) of the Convention.

Purpose of Limitation on Benefits Provisions

The United States views an income tax treaty as a vehicle for providing treaty benefits to residents of the two Contracting States. This statement begs the question of who is to be treated as a resident of a Contracting State for the purpose of being granted treaty benefits. The Commentaries to the OECD Model authorize a tax authority to deny benefits, under substance-over-form principles, to a nominee in one State deriving income from the other on behalf of a third-State resident. In addition, although the text of the OECD Model does not contain express anti-abuse provisions, the Commentary to Article 1 contains an extensive discussion approving the use of such provisions in tax treaties in order to limit the ability of third-State residents to obtain treaty benefits. The United States holds strongly to the view that tax treaties should include provisions that specifically prevent misuse of treaties by residents of third countries. Consequently, all recent U.S. income tax treaties contain comprehensive Limitation on Benefits provisions.

A treaty that provides treaty benefits to any resident of a Contracting State permits "treaty shopping": the use, by residents of third States, of legal entities established in a Contracting

State with a principal purpose to obtain the benefits of a tax treaty between the United States and the other Contracting State. It is important to note that this definition of treaty shopping does not encompass every case in which a third State resident establishes an entity in a U.S. treaty partner, and that entity enjoys treaty benefits to which the third State resident would not itself be entitled. If the third State resident had substantial reasons for establishing the structure that were unrelated to obtaining treaty benefits, then the structure would not fall within the definition of treaty shopping set forth above.

Of course, the fundamental problem presented by this approach is that it is based on the taxpayer's motives in establishing an entity in a particular country, which a tax administrator is normally ill-equipped to identify. In order to avoid the necessity of making this subjective determination Article 16, as amended by the Protocol, sets forth a series of objective tests. The assumption underlying each of these tests is that a taxpayer that satisfies the requirements of the test probably has a real business purpose for the structure it has adopted, or has a sufficiently strong nexus to the other Contracting State (*e.g.*, a resident individual) to warrant benefits even in the absence of a business connection, and that this business purpose or connection is sufficient to justify the conclusion that obtaining the benefits of the treaty is not a principal purpose of establishing or maintaining residence in that other State.

For instance, the assumption underlying the active trade or business test under paragraph (3) is that a third country resident that establishes a "substantial" operation in Australia and that derives income from a similar activity in the United States would not do so primarily to avail itself of the benefits of the Convention; it is presumed in such a case that the investor had a valid business purpose for investing in Australia, and that the link between that trade or business and the U.S. activity that generates the treaty-benefited income manifests a business purpose for placing the U.S. investments in the entity in Australia. It is considered unlikely that the investor would incur the expense of establishing a substantial trade or business in Australia simply to obtain the benefits of the Convention. A similar rationale underlies other tests in Article 16.

While these tests provide useful surrogates for identifying actual intent, these mechanical tests cannot account for every case in which the taxpayer is not treaty shopping. Accordingly, Article 16 also includes a provision (paragraph (5)) authorizing the competent authority of a Contracting State to grant benefits. While an analysis under paragraph (5) may well differ from that under one of the other tests of Article 16, its objective is the same: to identify investors whose residence in the other State can be justified by factors other than a purpose to derive treaty benefits.

Article 16 and the anti-abuse provisions of domestic law complement each other, as Article 16 effectively determines whether an entity has a sufficient nexus to the Contracting State to be treated as a resident for treaty purposes, while domestic anti-abuse provisions (*e.g.*, business purpose, substance-over-form, step transaction or conduit principles) determine whether a particular transaction should be recast in accordance with its substance. Thus, internal law principles of the source State may be applied to identify the beneficial owner of an item of income, and Article 16 then will be applied to the beneficial owner to determine if that person is entitled to the benefits of the Convention with respect to such income.

Article 16 limits benefits otherwise provided by other articles of the Convention. Thus, even though a resident of a Contracting State meets the requirements of Article 16, the resident is eligible for treaty benefits only if the resident satisfies any other specified conditions for claiming benefits. This means, for example, that a publicly-traded company that satisfies the conditions of sub-paragraph (2)(c) will be eligible for the zero rate of withholding tax on dividends at source only if it also satisfies the 12-month holding requirement of paragraph (3) of Article 10 (Dividends).

Structure of the Article

Article 16 generally follows the form used in other recent U.S. income tax treaties. Paragraph (1) states the general rule that a resident of a Contracting State is entitled to benefits otherwise accorded to residents only to the extent that the resident satisfies the requirements of the Article. Paragraph (2) lists a series of attributes of a resident of a Contracting State, any one of which suffices to make such resident a "qualified person" and thus entitled to all the benefits of the Convention. Paragraph (3) sets forth the active trade or business test, under which a person not entitled to benefits under paragraph (2) may nonetheless be granted benefits with regard to certain types of income. Paragraph (4) limits the benefits available under the other provisions of the Article in certain cases involving the issuance of "tracking stock" and similar instruments. Paragraph (5) provides that benefits may also be granted if the competent authority of the State from which the benefits are claimed determines that it is appropriate to grant benefits in that case. Paragraph (6) defines the terms used specifically in this Article. Paragraph (7) provides that the Article does not restrict either State from enforcing any anti-avoidance rule of its tax laws.

Paragraph 1

Paragraph (1) provides that, except as otherwise provided, a resident of a Contracting State will not be entitled to the benefits of the Convention otherwise accorded to residents of a Contracting State unless the resident is a "qualified person" as defined in paragraph (2) of Article 16.

The benefits otherwise accorded to residents under the Convention include all limitations on source-based taxation under Articles 6 through 15 and 17 through 21, the treaty-based relief from double taxation provided by Article 22 (Relief from Double Taxation), and the protection afforded to residents of a Contracting State under Article 23 (Non-discrimination). Some provisions do not require that a person be a resident in order to enjoy the benefits of those provisions. For example, Article 26 (Diplomatic and Consular Privileges) applies to diplomatic and consular privileges regardless of residence. Article 16 accordingly does not limit the availability of treaty benefits provided under these such provisions.

Paragraph 2

Paragraph (2) has eight sub-paragraphs, each describing a category of residents that constitute "qualified persons" and thus are entitled to all benefits of the Convention provided that they otherwise satisfy the requirements for a particular benefit. It is intended that the provisions of paragraph (2) will be self-executing. Claiming benefits under paragraph (2) does not require advance competent authority ruling or approval. The tax authorities may, of course, on review, determine that the taxpayer has improperly interpreted the paragraph and is not entitled to the benefits claimed.

Individuals -- Sub-paragraph (2)(a)

Sub-paragraph (a) provides that individual residents of a Contracting State will be entitled to all treaty benefits. If such an individual receives income as a nominee on behalf of a third country resident, benefits may be denied under the respective articles of the Convention by the requirement that the beneficial owner of the income be a resident of a Contracting State.

Governmental Entities -- Sub-paragraph (2)(b)

Sub-paragraph (b) provides that the Contracting State, any political subdivision or local authority of the State, or any agency or instrumentality of the State will be entitled to all benefits of the Convention.

Publicly-Traded Corporations -- Sub-paragraph (2)(c)

Sub-paragraph (c) of paragraph (2) applies to two categories of companies: publicly traded companies and subsidiaries of publicly traded companies. Clause (i) of sub-paragraph (c) generally provides that a company will be a qualified person if the principal class of its shares is listed on a recognized U.S. or Australian stock exchange and is regularly traded on one or more recognized stock exchanges. The term "recognized stock exchange" is defined in paragraph (6) as (a) the NASDAQ System owned by the National Association of Securities Dealers and any stock exchange registered with the Securities and Exchange Commission as a national securities exchange for purposes of the Securities Exchange Act of 1934, (b) the Australian Stock Exchange and any other Australian stock exchange recognized as such under Australian law, and (c) any other stock exchange agreed upon by the competent authorities of the Contracting States.

The term "principal class of shares" is not defined in the Convention. In accordance with paragraph (2) of Article 3 (General Definitions), this term will be defined by reference to the domestic tax laws of the State from which treaty benefits are sought, generally the source State. Generally, under U.S. tax law, the "principal class of shares" is defined as the common shares of the company representing the majority of the aggregate voting power and value of the company. If the company does not have a class of ordinary or common shares representing the majority of the aggregate voting power and value of the company, then the "principal class of shares" is that class or any combination of classes of shares that represents, in the aggregate, a majority of the voting power and value of the company. "Shares" include depository receipts for shares or trust certificates for shares.

The term "regularly traded" is not defined in the Convention. In accordance with paragraph (2) of Article 3 (General Definitions), this term will be defined by reference to the domestic tax laws of the State from which treaty benefits are sought, generally the source State. In the case of the United States, this term is understood to have the meaning it has under Treas.

Reg. section 1.884-5(d)(4)(i)(B), relating to the branch tax provisions of the Code. Under these regulations, a class of shares is considered to be "regularly traded" if two requirements are met: trades in the class of shares are made in more than de minimis quantities on at least 60 days during the taxable year, and the aggregate number of shares in the class traded during the year is at least 10 percent of the average number of shares outstanding during the year. Sections 1.884-5(d)(4)(i)(A), (ii) and (iii) will not be taken into account for purposes of defining the term "regularly traded" under the Convention.

The regular trading requirement can be met by trading on any recognized exchange or exchanges located in either State. Trading on one or more recognized stock exchanges may be aggregated for purposes of this requirement. Thus, a U.S. company could satisfy the regularly traded requirement through trading, in whole or in part, on a recognized stock exchange located in Australia or on a stock exchange in a third country (if agreed upon by the competent authorities). Authorized but unissued shares are not considered for purposes of this test.

A company resident in a Contracting State is entitled to the benefits of the Convention under clause (ii) of sub-paragraph (c) of paragraph (2) if five or fewer direct and indirect owners of at least 50 percent of the aggregate vote and value of the company's shares are publicly traded companies described in clause (i). Thus, for example, an Australian company, all the shares of which are owned by another Australian company, would qualify for benefits under the treaty if the principal class of shares of the Australian parent company were listed on the Australian Stock Exchange and regularly traded on a recognized U.S. or Australian stock exchange. However, the Australian company would not qualify for benefits under clause (ii) if the publicly traded parent company were a resident of Canada, not of the United States or Australia. Furthermore, if the Australian parent indirectly owned the Australian company through a chain of subsidiaries, each such subsidiary in the chain, as an intermediate owner, must be a resident of the United States or Australia for the Australian company to meet the test in clause (ii).

This test differs from that under sub-paragraph (c)(i) of paragraph (2) in that 50 percent of each class of the company's shares, not merely the class or classes accounting for more than 50 percent of the company's votes and value, must be held by publicly-traded companies described in paragraph (2)(c)(i). Thus, the test under paragraph 2(c)(ii) considers the ownership of every class of shares outstanding, while the test under paragraph 2(c)(i) only considers those classes that account for a majority of the company's voting power and value. However, both subparagraphs are subject to the rules of paragraph (4), relating to certain arrangements pursuant to which holders of a class of stock in a resident of a Contracting State receive a disproportionate share of the income arising from the other Contracting State.

The rules of paragraph (4) may interact with the rules of this paragraph in order to deny benefits in whole or in part. The following example illustrates this interaction.

Example. AusCo is a corporation resident in Australia. AusCo has two classes of shares: Common and Preferred. The Common shares are listed on the Australian Stock Exchange and are substantially and regularly traded. The Preferred shares have no voting rights and are entitled to receive dividends equal in amount to interest payments that AusCo receives from unrelated borrowers in the United States. The Preferred shares are owned entirely by a single investor that is a resident of a country with which the United States does not have a tax treaty. The Common shares account for more than 50 percent of the value of AusCo and for 100 percent of the voting power. Because the owner of the Preferred shares is entitled to receive payments corresponding to the U.S. source interest income earned by AusCo, the Preferred shares are subject to the rules of paragraph 4. Because the owner of the Preferred shares is not a "qualified person," AusCo will be denied benefits with respect to a portion of the interest payments. Benefits will be denied to the extent that the owner of the Preferred shares receives a greater proportion of the U.S. income than he would have received had he owned comparable Common shares.

Publicly-Traded Persons -- Sub-paragraph (2)(d)

Sub-paragraph (d) of paragraph (2) applies to two categories of persons that are not individuals or companies under the laws of one of the Contracting States: publicly traded entities and entities owned either by publicly traded companies or by publicly traded entities that are not companies. Clause (i) of sub-paragraph (d) provides that a person other than a company will be a qualified person if the principal class of units in that person is listed on a recognized U.S. or Australian stock exchange and is regularly traded on one or more recognized stock exchanges.

A person other than an individual or a company is a qualified person under clause (ii) of sub-paragraph (d) if the direct or indirect owners of at least fifty percent of the beneficial interests in the entity are entities that satisfy the publicly traded test of sub-paragraphs (c) or (d). Thus, for example, an Australian trust, a majority of the shares of ownership in which are owned by a second Australian trust, would be a qualified person if the principal class of units of the second Australian trust were listed on the Australian Stock Exchange and regularly traded on the U.S. Stock Exchange. However, the first Australian trust would not qualify for benefits under clause (ii) if the second Australian trust were a resident of Japan, not of the United States or the Australia.

Sub-paragraph (d) applies generally to trusts the shares of ownership in which are publicly traded and to trusts that are owned by publicly traded entities. From the U.S. perspective, this provision relating to publicly traded trusts is redundant, since the United States would generally consider such trusts to be companies covered by the parallel provision under sub-paragraph (c).

The rules of paragraph (4) may interact with the rules of this paragraph in order to deny benefits in whole or in part. The following example illustrates this interaction.

Example 1. AUIT1 is an Australian unit investment trust that was organized to invest in U.S. stocks. It is one of a family of unit investment trusts organized by the same investment manager, each of which invests in stocks of a single country. Investors who want a diversified global portfolio invest in AUIT2, a unit investment trust that holds a controlling interest in each of the individual country funds and is regularly traded on the Australian Stock Exchange. AUIT2 owns 60% of AUIT1's outstanding units; the rest are widely held. AUIT1 qualifies for benefits.

Example 2. AUIT1 is an Australian unit investment trust that holds a diversified global portfolio of stocks. AUIT2 is a unit investment trust that owns 60% of the units in AUIT1. AUIT2 issues a number of classes of units to accommodate the investment strategies of its unitholders. It lists all of its classes of units on the Australian Stock Exchange and meets the regular trading test. One class of units tracks the performance of a portfolio of U.S. technology companies. Because AUIT2 controls AUIT1, and the holders of that class of units will receive a disproportionate share of AUIT1's income from U.S. sources, paragraph (4) will apply. Accordingly, AUIT1 will be denied benefits with respect to a portion of the income received with respect to the technology companies in the portfolio if a majority of that class of shares is owned by persons who are qualified persons.

Tax Exempt Organizations -- Sub-paragraph (2)(e)

Sub-paragraph (e) of paragraph (2) provides that certain tax-exempt organizations will be "qualified persons." Entities qualifying under this sub-paragraph are those that are organized under U.S. or Australian law and established and maintained in the State of residence exclusively for religious, charitable, educational, scientific, or similar purposes. These entities are generally exempt from tax in their State of residence. There is no requirement that specified percentages of the beneficiaries of these organizations be residents of one of the Contracting States.

Pension Funds -- Sub-paragraph (2)(f)

Sub-paragraph (f) of paragraph (2) provides that certain pension funds will be "qualified persons." An entity qualifying under this sub-paragraph is one that is organized under U.S. or Australian law and established and maintained in the State of residence to provide, pursuant to a plan, pensions or other similar benefits to employed and self-employed persons. For the entity to be a qualified person, however, more than fifty percent of the entity's beneficiaries, members or participants must be individuals resident in either Contracting State. For purposes of this provision, the term "beneficiaries" should be understood to refer to the persons receiving benefits from the organization. The entity need not be taxed in its State of residence.

Ownership/Base Erosion -- Sub-paragraph (2)(g)

Sub-paragraph (2)(g) provides a two-part test, the so-called ownership and base erosion test. This test applies to any form of legal entity that is a resident of a Contracting State. Both prongs of the test must be satisfied for the resident to be entitled to benefits under sub-paragraph (2)(g).

The ownership prong of the test, under clause (i), requires that 50 percent or more of the aggregate voting power and value of the person be owned directly or indirectly on at least half the days of the person's taxable year by persons who are themselves qualified persons under certain other tests of paragraph (2)—sub-paragraphs (a) or (b), or clause (i) of sub-paragraphs (c) or (d).

Trusts may be entitled to benefits under this provision if they are treated as residents under Article 4 (Residence) and they otherwise satisfy the requirements of this sub-paragraph.

27

For purposes of this sub-paragraph, the beneficial interests in a trust will be considered to be owned by its beneficiaries in proportion to each beneficiary's actuarial interest in the trust. The interest of a remainder beneficiary will be equal to 100 percent less the aggregate percentages held by income beneficiaries. A beneficiary's interest in a trust will not be considered to be owned by a person entitled to benefits under the other provisions of paragraph (2) if it is not possible to determine the beneficiary's actuarial interest. Consequently, if it is not possible to determine the actuarial interest of any beneficiaries in a trust, the ownership test under clause (i) cannot be satisfied, unless all possible beneficiaries are persons entitled to benefits under the other sub-paragraphs of paragraph (2).

The base erosion prong of clause (ii) of sub-paragraph (g) disqualifies a person if fifty percent or more of the person's gross income for the taxable year is paid or accrued to a person or persons who are not residents of either Contracting State in the form of payments deductible for tax purposes in the payer's State of residence.

The term "gross income" is not defined in the Convention. Thus, in accordance with paragraph (2) of Article 3 (General Definitions), in determining whether a person deriving income from United States sources is entitled to the benefits of the Convention, the United States will ascribe the meaning to the term that it has in the United States. In the case of the United States, the term "gross income" has the same meaning as such term in section 61 of the Code and the regulations thereunder.

To the extent they are deductible from the taxable base, trust distributions are deductible payments. However, depreciation and amortization deductions, which do not represent payments or accruals to other persons, are disregarded for this purpose. Deductible payments also do not include arm's length payments in the ordinary course of business for services or tangible property or payments in respect of financial obligations to banks that are residents of either Contracting State, or that have a permanent establishment in either Contracting State to which the payment is attributable.

The rules of paragraph (4) may interact with the rules of this paragraph as they apply to companies in order to deny benefits in whole or in part. The following example illustrates this interaction.

Example. A group of Australian resident individuals established an investment club. The investment club purchases stocks through HoldCo, an Australian company owned by the Australian resident individuals in proportion to their contributions to the investment club. The rules of the investment club prevent the club from borrowing. One of the club's investments was an 80% interest in a U.S. biotech company, USCo. USCo developed an unusual gene therapy, resulting in a substantial increase in the value of USCo stock. The members of the club wanted to sell some of the shares of USCo in order to diversify their holdings, but did not want to be subject to capital gains tax in Australia. Instead, HoldCo issued a class of preferred shares that track the dividends paid by USCo to HoldCo in exchange for a capital contribution from Investor. Investor is an individual resident in a third country. HoldCo meets the test for eligibility for the 5 percent maximum rate of withholding tax under paragraph 2(a) of Article 10. However, HoldCo would not be entitled to the five percent maximum rate of withholding tax on a portion of the dividends paid by USCo to the extent the preferred shares result in Investor receiving a disproportionate part of the income of HoldCo.

Headquarters company test – Sub-paragraph (2)(h)

Sub-paragraph (2)(h) provides that a resident of one of the Contracting States is entitled to all the benefits of the Convention if that person functions as a recognized headquarters company for a multinational corporate group. For this purpose, the multinational corporate group includes all corporations that the headquarters company supervises and excludes affiliated corporations not supervised by the headquarters company. The headquarters company does not have to own shares in the companies that it supervises. In order to be considered a headquarters company, the person must meet several requirements that are enumerated in sub-paragraph (2)(h). These requirements are discussed below.

Overall Supervision and Administration

Clause (2)(h)(i) provides that the person must provide a substantial portion of the overall supervision and administration of the group. This activity may include group financing, but group financing may not be the principal activity of the person functioning as the headquarters company. A person only will be considered to engage in supervision and administration if it engages in a number of the following activities: group financing, pricing, marketing, internal auditing, internal communications, and management. Other activities also could be part of the function of supervision and administration.

In determining whether a "substantial portion" of the overall supervision and administration of the group is provided by the headquarters company, its headquarters-related activities must be substantial in relation to the same activities for the same group performed by other entities.

Clause (2)(h)(i) does not require that the group that is supervised include persons in the other State. However, it is anticipated that in most cases the group will include such persons, due to the requirement discussed below that the income derived by the headquarters company be derived in connection with or be incidental to an active trade or business supervised by the headquarters company.

Active Trade or Business

Clause (2)(h)(ii) is the first of several requirements intended to ensure that the relevant group is truly "multinational." This sub-paragraph provides that the corporate group supervised by the headquarters company must consist of corporations resident in, and engaged in active trades or businesses in, at least five countries. Furthermore, at least five countries must contribute substantially to the income generated by the group, as the rule requires that the business activities carried on in each of the five countries (or groupings of countries) generate at least 10 percent of the gross income of the group. For purposes of the 10 percent gross income requirement, the income from multiple countries may be aggregated, as long as there are at least five individual countries or groupings that each satisfy the 10 percent requirement. If the gross income requirement under this clause is not met for a taxable year, the taxpayer may satisfy this requirement by averaging the ratios for the four years preceding the taxable year.

Example 1. AHQ is a corporation resident in Australia. AHQ functions as a headquarters company for a group of companies. These companies are resident in the United States, Canada, New Zealand, the United Kingdom, Malaysia, the Philippines, Singapore, and Indonesia. The gross income generated by each of these companies for 2004 and 2005 is as follows:

Country	2004	2005
United States	$40	$45
Canada	$25	$15
New Zealand	$10	$20
United Kingdom	$30	$35
Malaysia	$10	$12
Philippines	$ 7	$10
Singapore	$10	$ 8
Indonesia	$ 5	$10
	$137	$155

For 2004, 10 percent of the gross income of this group is equal to $13.70. Only the United States, Canada, and the United Kingdom satisfy this requirement for that year. The other companies in the group may be aggregated to meet this requirement. Because New Zealand and Malaysia have a total gross income of $20, and the Philippines, Singapore, and Indonesia have a total gross income of $22, these two groupings of countries may be treated as the fourth and fifth members of the group for purposes of clause (2)(h)(ii).

In the following year, 10 percent of the gross income is $15.50. Only the United States, New Zealand, and the United Kingdom satisfy this requirement. Because Canada and Malaysia have a total gross income of $27, and the Philippines, Singapore, and Indonesia have a total gross income of $28, these two groupings of countries may be treated as the fourth and fifth members of the group for purposes of clause (2)(h)(ii). The fact that Canada replaced New Zealand in a group not relevant for this purpose. The composition of the grouping may change from year to year.

Single Country Limitation

Clause (2)(h)(iii) provides that the business activities carried on in any one country other than the headquarters company's state of residence must generate less than 50 percent of the gross income of the group. If the gross income requirement under this clause is not met for a taxable year, the taxpayer may satisfy this requirement by averaging the ratios for the four years preceding the taxable year. The following example illustrates the application of this subparagraph.

Example. AHQ is a corporation resident in Australia. AHQ functions as a headquarters company for a group of companies. AHQ derives dividend income from a United States subsidiary in the 2004 taxable year. The state of residence of each of these companies, the situs of their activities and the amounts of gross income attributable to each for the years 2004 through 2008 are set forth below.

Company	Situs	2008	2007	2006	2005	2004
United States	U.S.	$100	$100	$ 95	$ 90	$ 85
United States	Mexico	10	8	5	0	0
United States	Canada	20	18	16	15	12
United Kingdom	U.K	30	32	30	28	27
New Zealand	N.Z.	40	42	38	36	35
Japan	Japan	35	32	30	30	28
Singapore	Singapore	25	25	24	22	20
		$260	$257	$238	$221	$207

Because the United States' total gross income of $130 in 2007 is not less than 50 percent of the gross income of the group, clause (2)(h)(iii) is not satisfied with respect to dividends derived in 2007. However, the United States' average gross income for the preceding four years may be used in lieu of the preceding year's average. The United States' average gross income for the years 2004-07 is $111.00 ($444/4). The group's total average gross income for these years is $230.75 ($923/4). Because $111.00 represents 48.1 percent of the group's average gross income for the years 2004 through 2007, the requirement under clause (2)(h)(iii) is satisfied.

Other State Gross Income Limitation

Clause (2)(h)(iv) provides that no more than 25 percent of the headquarters company's gross income may be derived from the other Contracting State. Thus, if the headquarters company's gross income for the taxable year is $200, no more than $50 of this amount may be derived from the other Contracting State. If the gross income requirement under this clause is not met for a taxable year, the taxpayer may satisfy this requirement by averaging the ratios for the four years preceding the taxable year.

Independent Discretionary Authority

Clause (2)(h)(v) requires that the headquarters company have and exercise independent discretionary authority to carry out the functions referred to in clause (i). Thus, if the headquarters company was nominally responsible for group financing, pricing, marketing and other management functions, but merely implemented instructions received from another entity, the headquarters company would not be considered to have and exercise independent discretionary authority with respect to these functions. This determination is made individually for each function. For instance, a headquarters company could be nominally responsible for group financing, pricing, marketing and internal auditing functions, but another entity could be actually directing the headquarters company as to the group financing function. In such a case, the headquarters company would not be deemed to have independent discretionary authority for group financing, but it might have such authority for the other functions. Functions for which the headquarters company does not have and exercise independent discretionary authority are considered to be conducted by an entity other than the headquarters company for purposes of clause (i).

Income Taxation Rules

Clause (2)(h)(vi) requires that the headquarters company be subject to the generally applicable income taxation rules in its country of residence. This reference should be understood to mean that the company must be subject to the income taxation rules to which a company engaged in the active conduct of a trade or business would be subject. Thus, if one of the Contracting States introduced special taxation legislation that would impose a lower rate of income tax on headquarters companies than was imposed on companies engaged in the active conduct of a trade or business, or would provide for an artificially low taxable base for such companies, a headquarters company subject to these rules would not be entitled to the benefits of the Convention under sub-paragraph (2)(h).

In Connection With or Incidental to Trade or Business

Finally, clause (2)(h)(vii) requires that the income derived in the other Contracting State be derived in connection with or be incidental to the active business activities referred to in clause (ii). This determination is made under the principles set forth in paragraph (3). For instance, if an Australian company that satisfied the other requirements in sub-paragraph (2)(h) acted as a headquarters company for a group that included a United States corporation, and the group was engaged in the design and manufacture of computer software, but the U.S. company was also engaged in the design and manufacture of photocopying machines, the income that the Australian company derived from the United States would have to be derived in connection with or be incidental to the income generated by the computer business in order to be entitled to the benefits of the Convention under sub-paragraph (2)(h). Interest income received from the U.S. company also would be entitled to the benefits of the Convention under this paragraph as long as the interest was attributable to a trade or business supervised by the headquarters company. Interest income derived from an unrelated party would normally not, however, satisfy the requirements of this clause.

The rules of paragraph (4) may interact with the rules of this paragraph as they apply to companies in order to deny benefits in whole or in part.

Paragraph 3

Paragraph (3) sets forth a test under which a resident of a Contracting State that is not a "qualified person" under paragraph (2) may receive treaty benefits with respect to certain items of income that are connected to an active trade or business conducted in its State of residence.

Sub-paragraph (a) sets forth the general rule that a resident of a Contracting State engaged in the active conduct of a trade or business in that State may obtain the benefits of the Convention with respect to an item of income derived in the other Contracting State. The item of income, however, must be derived in connection with or be incidental to that trade or business.

The term "trade or business" is not defined in the Convention. Pursuant to paragraph (2) of Article 3 (General Definitions), when determining whether a resident of Australia is entitled to the benefits of the Convention under paragraph (3) of this Article with respect to an item of income derived from sources within the United States, the United States will ascribe to this term the meaning that it has under the law of the United States. Accordingly, the U.S. competent authority will refer to the regulations issued under section 367(a) for the definition of the term "trade or business." In general, therefore, a trade or business will be considered to be a specific unified group of activities that constitute or could constitute an independent economic enterprise carried on for profit. Furthermore, a corporation generally will be considered to carry on a trade or business only if the officers and employees of the corporation conduct substantial managerial and operational activities.

The business of making or managing investments for the resident's own account will be considered to be a trade or business only when such activities are part of banking, insurance or securities activities conducted by a bank, an insurance company, or a registered, licensed or authorized securities dealer. Such activities conducted by a person other than a bank, insurance company or registered, licensed or authorized securities dealer will not be considered to be the conduct of an active trade or business, nor would they be considered to be the conduct of an active trade or business if conducted by a bank, insurance company or registered, licensed or authorized securities dealer but not as part of the company's banking, insurance or dealer business.

Because a headquarters operation is in the business of managing investments, a company that functions solely as a headquarters company will not be considered to be engaged in an active trade or business for purposes of sub-paragraph (a).

For purposes of this paragraph, income is derived in connection with a trade or business if the income-producing activity in the State of source is a line of business that forms a part of or is complementary to the trade or business conducted in the State of residence by the income recipient. A business activity generally will be considered to "form a part of" a business activity conducted in the other State if the two activities involve the design, manufacture or sale of the same products or type of products, or the provision of similar services. The line of business in the State of residence may be upstream, downstream, or parallel to the activity conducted in the State of source. Thus, the line of business may provide inputs for a manufacturing process that occurs in the State of source, may sell the output of that manufacturing process, or simply may sell the same sorts of products that are being sold by the trade or business carried on in the State of source.

In order for two activities to be considered to be "complementary," the activities need not relate to the same types of products or services, but they should be part of the same overall industry and be related in the sense that the success or failure of one activity will tend to result in success or failure for the other. In cases in which more than one trade or business is conducted in the other State and only one of the trades or businesses forms a part of or is complementary to a trade or business conducted in the State of residence, it is necessary to identify the trade or business to which an item of income is attributable. Royalties generally will be considered to be derived in connection with the trade or business to which the underlying intangible property is attributable. Dividends will be deemed to be derived first out of earnings and profits of the treaty-benefited trade or business, and then out of other earnings and profits. Interest income may be allocated under any reasonable method consistently applied. A method that conforms to U.S. principles for expense allocation will be considered a reasonable method. The following examples illustrate the application of this rule.

Example 1. USCo is a corporation resident in the United States. USCo is engaged in an active manufacturing business in the United States. USCo owns 100 percent of the shares of AusCo, a corporation resident in Australia. AusCo distributes USCo products in Australia. Because the business activities conducted by the two corporations involve the same products, AusCo's distribution business is considered to form a part of USCo's manufacturing business.

Example 2. The facts are the same as in Example 1, except that USCo does not manufacture. Rather, USCo operates a large research and development facility in the United States that licenses intellectual property to affiliates worldwide, including AusCo. AusCo and other USCo affiliates then manufacture and market the USCo-designed products in their respective markets. Because the activities conducted by AusCo and USCo involve the same product lines, these activities are considered to form a part of the same trade or business.

Example 3. Americair is a corporation resident in the United States that operates an international airline. AusSub is a wholly-owned subsidiary of Americair resident in Australia. AusSub operates a chain of hotels in Australia that are located near airports served by Americair flights. Americair frequently sells tour packages that include air travel to Australia and lodging at AusSub hotels. Although both companies are engaged in the active conduct of a trade or business, the businesses of operating a chain of hotels and operating an airline are distinct trades or businesses. Therefore AusSub's business does not form a part of Americair's business. However, AusSub's business is considered to be complementary to Americair's business because they are part of the same overall industry (travel) and the links between their operations tend to make them interdependent.

Example 4. The facts are the same as in Example 3, except that AusSub owns an office building in Australia instead of a hotel chain. No part of Americair's business is conducted through the office building. AusSub's business is not considered to form a part of or to be complementary to Americair's business. They are engaged in distinct trades or businesses in separate industries, and there is no economic dependence between the two operations.

Example 5. USFlower is a corporation resident in the United States. USFlower produces and sells flowers in the United States and other countries. USFlower owns all the shares of AusHolding, a corporation resident in Australia. AusHolding is a holding company that is not engaged in a trade or business. AusHolding owns all the shares of three corporations that are resident in Australia: AusFlower, AusLawn, and AusFish. AusFlower distributes USFlower flowers under the USFlower trademark in Australia. AusLawn markets a line of lawn care products in Australia under the USFlower trademark. In addition to being sold under the same trademark, AusLawn and AusFlower products are sold in the same stores and sales of each company's products tend to generate increased sales of the other's products. AusFish imports fish from the United States and distributes it to fish wholesalers in Australia. For purposes of paragraph (3), the business of AusFlower forms a part of the business of USFlower, the business of AusLawn is complementary to the business of USFlower, and the business of AusFish is neither part of nor complementary to that of USFlower.

Finally, a resident in one of the States also will be entitled to the benefits of the Convention with respect to income derived from the other State if the income is "incidental" to the trade or business conducted in the recipient's State of residence. Income derived from a State will be incidental to a trade or business conducted in the other State if the production of such income facilitates the conduct of the trade or business in the other State. An example of incidental income is the temporary investment of working capital of a person in the State of residence in securities issued by persons in the State of source.

Sub-paragraph (b) of paragraph (3) states a further condition to the general rule in sub-paragraph (a) in cases where the trade or business generating the item of income in question is carried on either by the person deriving the income or by any associated enterprises. Sub-paragraph (b) states that the trade or business carried on in the State of residence, under these circumstances, must be substantial in relation to the activity in the State of source. This determination is made based upon all the facts and circumstances and takes into account the comparative sizes of the trades or businesses in each Contracting State (measured by reference to asset values, income and payroll expenses), the nature of the activities performed in each Contracting State, and the relative contributions made to that trade or business in each Contracting State. In making each determination or comparison, due regard will be given to the relative sizes of the U.S. and Australian economies.

The determination in sub-paragraph (b) also is made separately for each item of income derived from the State of source. It therefore is possible that a person would be entitled to the benefits of the Convention with respect to one item of income but not with respect to another. If a resident of a Contracting State is entitled to treaty benefits with respect to a particular item of income under paragraph (3), the resident is entitled to all benefits of the Convention insofar as they affect the taxation of that item of income in the State of source.

The substantiality requirement is intended to prevent a narrow case of treaty-shopping abuses in which a company attempts to qualify for benefits by engaging in de minimis connected business activities in the treaty country in which it is resident (*i.e.*, activities that have little economic cost or effect with respect to the company business as a whole).

The application of the substantiality test only to income from related parties focuses only on potential abuse cases, and does not hamper certain other kinds of non-abusive activities, even though the income recipient resident in a Contracting State may be very small in relation to the entity generating income in the other Contracting State. For example, if a small U.S. research firm develops a process that it licenses to a very large, unrelated Australian manufacturer, the size of the U.S. research firm would not be tested against the size of the Australian manufacturer. Similarly, a small U.S. bank that makes a loan to a very large unrelated Australian business would not have to pass a substantiality test to receive treaty benefits under sub-paragraph (b).

Sub-paragraph (c) of paragraph (3) provides special rules for determining whether a resident of a Contracting State is engaged in the active conduct of a trade or business within the meaning of sub-paragraph (a). Sub-paragraph (c) attributes the activities of a partnership to each of its partners. Sub-paragraph (c) also attributes to a person activities conducted by persons "connected" to such person. A person ("X") is connected to another person ("Y") if X possesses fifty percent or more of the beneficial interest in Y (or if Y possesses fifty percent or more of the beneficial interest in X). For this purpose, X is connected to a company if X owns shares representing fifty percent or more of the aggregate voting power and value of the company or fifty percent or more of the beneficial equity interest in the company. X also is connected to Y if a third person possesses fifty percent or more of the beneficial interest in both X and Y. For this purpose, if X or Y is a company, the threshold relationship with respect to such company or companies is fifty percent or more of the aggregate vote and value or fifty percent or more of the beneficial equity interest. Finally, X is connected to Y if, based upon all the facts and circumstances, X controls Y, Y controls X, or X and Y are controlled by the same person or persons.

Paragraph 4

Paragraph (4) denies the benefits of the Convention to the disproportionate part of the income earned by certain companies. A company is subject to paragraph (4) if it meets two tests, set forth in sub-paragraphs (a) and (b) of paragraph (4). A company resident in a Contracting State meets the test of sub-paragraph (a) if it has outstanding a class of shares which is subject to terms or other arrangements which entitle the holder to a larger portion of the company's income derived from the other Contracting State than the holder otherwise would be entitled in the absence of such terms or arrangements. Thus, for example, a company resident in Australia meets the test of sub-paragraph (a) if it has outstanding a class of "tracking stock" that pays dividends based upon a formula that approximates the company's return on its assets employed in the United States.

The disproportionate part of the income of the company is the excess portion of the company's income from the other Contracting State to which the holders are entitled, above what they otherwise would be entitled. So-called alphabet stock that entitles the holder to earnings in the State produced by a particular division of the company would cause a company to be subject to the rule of paragraph (4).

Example 1. AusCo is a company resident in Australia that specializes in food products. AusCo has two classes of shares: Common and Class S Common. The Common shares are listed on the Australian Stock Exchange and are substantially and regularly traded. Class S Common is so-called tracking stock. The dividends on Class S Common are equal to the earnings and profits of Software Co., a U.S. subsidiary of AusCo. Dividends cannot be paid on Class S shares if AusCo does not have sufficient earnings and profits; otherwise, the return on Class S shares is independent of the performance of AusCo's food business. The Class S shares were created by AusCo because it felt that the stock market did not appropriately value the contribution that Software Co. made to the AusCo group. Because the holders of the Class S Common shares are entitled to receive payments corresponding to the earnings and profits of

Software Co., a U.S. company, AusCo is subject to paragraph 4 with respect to dividends received from Software Co.

Example 2. AusCo is a corporation resident in Australia. AusCo has two classes of shares: Common and Preferred. The Common shares are listed on the Australian Stock Exchange and are substantially and regularly traded. The Preferred shares have no voting rights and are entitled to receive dividends equal in amount to the income earned by AusCo from selling widgets in Australia. Because the Preferred shares do not entitle the owner to receive dividends or other payments corresponding to U.S.-source income received by AusCo, the Preferred shares are not considered a disproportionate class of shares.

A company meets the test of sub-paragraph (b) if fifty percent or more of the voting power and value of the class of shares is owned by persons who are not "qualified persons."

Paragraph 5

Paragraph (5) provides that a resident of one of the Contracting States that is neither a qualified person nor entitled to the benefits of the Convention with respect to an item of income under paragraph (3) of this Article still may be granted benefits under the Convention at the discretion of the competent authority of the State from which benefits are claimed. In making determinations under paragraph 6, that competent authority will take into account as its guideline whether the establishment, acquisition or maintenance of the person seeking benefits under the Convention, or the conduct of such person's operations, has or had as one of its principal purposes the obtaining of benefits under the Convention. Thus, persons that establish operations in one of the Contracting States with a principal purpose of obtaining the benefits of the Convention ordinarily will not be granted relief under paragraph (5).

The competent authority may determine to grant all benefits of the Convention, or it may determine to grant only certain benefits. For instance, it may determine to grant benefits only with respect to a particular item of income in a manner similar to paragraph (3). Further, the competent authority may set time limits on the duration of any relief granted.

For purposes of implementing paragraph (5), a taxpayer will be permitted to present his case to the relevant competent authority for an advance determination based on the facts. In these circumstances, it is also expected that if the competent authority determines that benefits are to be allowed, they will be allowed retroactively to the time of entry into force of the relevant treaty provision or the establishment of the structure in question, whichever is later.

Paragraph 6

Paragraph (6) defines the term "recognized stock exchange." See the paragraph (2) discussion above.

Paragraph 7

Paragraph (7) provides that nothing in Article 16 restricts, in any manner, the ability of the Contracting States to enact and enforce anti-avoidance provisions in their tax laws.

Article 11

Article 11 of the Protocol replaces Article 21 (Other Income) of the Convention to make the language track the UN Model provision more closely.

Paragraph 1

Paragraph (1) generally assigns taxing jurisdiction over income not dealt with in the other articles (Articles 6 through 15 and 17 through 20) of the Convention to the State of residence of the beneficial owner of the income. An item of income is "dealt with" in another article if it is the type of income described in the article and it has its source in a Contracting State. For example, all royalty income that arises in a Contracting State and that is beneficially owned by a resident of the other Contracting State is "dealt with" in Article 12 (Royalties). Distributions from partnerships and distributions from trusts are not generally dealt with under Article 21 because partnership and trust distributions generally do not constitute income. Under the Code, partners include in income their distributive share of partnership income annually, and partnership distributions themselves generally do not give rise to income. Also, under the Code, trust income and distributions have the character of the associated distributable net income and therefore would generally be covered by another article of the Convention. See Code section 641 et seq.

The exclusive residence tax rule of paragraph (1), however, is substantially limited by paragraph (3).

Paragraph 2

This paragraph provides an exception to the general rule of paragraph (1) for income, other than income from real property, that is attributable to a permanent establishment or fixed base maintained in a Contracting State by a resident of the other Contracting State. The taxation of such income is governed by the provisions of Articles 7 (Business Profits) and 14 (Independent Personal Services). Therefore, income arising outside the United States that is attributable to a permanent establishment maintained in the United States by a resident of Australia generally would be taxable by the United States under the provisions of Article 7. This would be true even if the income is sourced in a third State.

Paragraph 3

Paragraph (3) is not found in the U.S. or OECD Models. It is taken from the U.N. Model. It provides that, notwithstanding paragraphs (1) and (2), items of income of a resident not dealt with in the other articles (Articles 6 through 15 and 17 through 20) of the Convention may also be taxed by the source State. Thus, gambling income of a resident of the United States that arises in Australia may be taxed both in the United States and in Australia. Under Article 22 (Relief from Double Taxation) of the Convention, the United States generally must give a credit for the tax paid to Australia on the gambling income. Paragraph (1), therefore, provides exclusive residence-based taxation only to income of a resident of one of the Contracting States that does not arise in the other Contracting State.

Relation to Other Articles

This Article is subject to the saving clause of paragraph (3) of Article 1 (Personal Scope). Thus, the United States may tax the income of a resident of Australia that is not dealt with elsewhere in the Convention, if that resident is a citizen of the United States. The Article is also subject to the provisions of Article 16 (Limitation on Benefits). Thus, if a resident of Australia earns income that falls within the scope of paragraph (1) of Article 21, Article 21 would exempt the income from U.S. tax only if the resident satisfies one of the tests of Article 16 for entitlement to benefits.

Article 12

Article 12 of the Protocol makes a conforming change to Article 22 (Relief from Double Taxation) of the Convention to reflect the modifications made by the Protocol to Article 2 (Taxes Covered) of the Convention. The effect of the change is to clarify that, for purposes of applying the U.S. foreign tax credit, only the Australian income tax, including the tax on capital gains, and not the RRT, shall be considered as income taxes. Accordingly, the United States will provide a credit for RRT only if it is creditable under U.S. domestic law.

Article 13

Article 13 relates to entry into force of the modifications made by the Protocol.

Paragraph 1

Paragraph (1) provides for the ratification of the Protocol by both Contracting States according to their constitutional and statutory requirements. Instruments of ratification shall be exchanged as soon as possible.

In the United States, the process leading to ratification and entry into force is as follows: Once a protocol or treaty has been signed by authorized representatives of the two Contracting

States, the Department of State sends the protocol or treaty to the President who formally transmits it to the Senate for its advice and consent to ratification, which requires approval by two-thirds of the Senators present and voting. Prior to this vote, however, it generally has been the practice for the Senate Committee on Foreign Relations to hold hearings on the protocol or treaty and make a recommendation regarding its approval to the full Senate. Both Government and private sector witnesses may testify at these hearings. After receiving the Senate's advice and consent to ratification, the protocol or treaty is returned to the President for his signature on the ratification document. The President's signature on the document completes the process in the United States.

Paragraph 2

Paragraph (2) provides that the Protocol is an integral part of the Convention and that it will enter into force upon the exchange of instruments of ratification. The date on which a protocol or treaty enters into force is not necessarily the date on which its provisions take effect. Paragraph (2), therefore, also contains rules that determine when the provisions of the Protocol will have effect. Sub-paragraph (a) provides when the Protocol will have effect with respect to Australian taxes, and sub-paragraph (b) provides when the Protocol will have effect with respect to U.S. taxes.

Clauses (a)(i) and (b)(i) provide that the provisions of the Protocol relating to withholding taxes on dividends, royalties and interest take effect on or after the later of (A) the first day of the second month following the date on which the Protocol enters into force or (B) July 1, 2003. For example, if instruments of ratification are exchanged on March 31, 2003, the rates of withholding tax specified in paragraph (2) and (3) of Article 10 (Dividends) would be applicable to any dividends paid or credited on or after July 1, 2003. On the other hand, if the instruments of ratification are exchanged on September 15, 2003, the rates of withholding tax specified in paragraph (2) and (3) of Article 10 would be applicable to dividends paid or credited on or after November 1, 2003. If for some reason a withholding agent withholds at a higher rate than that provided by the Protocol (perhaps because it was not able to re-program its computers before the payment is made), a beneficial owner of the income that is a resident of Australia may make a claim for refund pursuant to section 1464 of the Code.

With respect to other taxes, paragraph (2) specifies different effective dates for the United States and Australia. The different effective dates reflect the differences between the tax and accounting periods in each Contracting State. With respect to the United States, the Protocol will have effect for taxes (other than withholding taxes) with respect to income arising in any taxable period beginning on or after January 1 of the year following entry into force. With respect to Australia, the Protocol will have effect for taxes (other than withholding taxes) with respect to income arising in any year of income beginning on or after July 1st of the year following entry into force.

Paragraph 3

Paragraph (3) contains a special rule for certain REIT dividends received by an LAPT. In the case of REIT shares owned by an LAPT on March 26, 2001, or acquired by the LAPT pursuant to a binding contract entered into on or before March 26, 2001 ("grandfathered REIT shares"), dividends from the grandfathered REIT shares are subject to the provisions of Article 10 (Dividends) as in effect on March 26, 2001. Thus, the dividends from the grandfathered REIT shares will be subject to a maximum rate of withholding tax of 15 percent, regardless of the ownership of the LAPT. REIT shares acquired by the LAPT pursuant to a reinvestment of dividends (ordinary or capital) from grandfathered REIT shares are also treated as grandfathered REIT shares.

Absent this special rule, the rate of withholding tax applicable to the REIT dividends paid to the LAPT would depend upon the ownership of the LAPT. Under Article 10, as modified by the Protocol, if a unitholder owns 5 percent or more of the beneficial interests in the LAPT, a proportionate amount of the REIT dividends received by the LAPT may not be eligible for the 15 percent maximum rate of withholding tax. Rather, if the 5 percent or greater unitholder does not meet the requirements of paragraph (4)(c) of Article 10, as modified by the Protocol, then the portion of the REIT dividends paid to the LAPT equivalent to the unitholder's interest in the LAPT will be subject to U.S. withholding tax of 30 percent.

This special rule for REIT shares held by LAPTs is intended to protect existing investments in REITs by LAPTs. LAPTs get special benefits under Australian law, as do REITs under U.S. law. The purpose of this special treatment, for both REITs and LAPTs, is to encourage collective investment by small shareholders. Sub-paragraph (4)(d) is intended to replicate, as closely as possible, the tax treatment of direct investment by LAPT shareholders. On a going forward basis, sub-paragraph (4)(d) gives small shareholders the same benefits with respect to REIT shares that they would get if they held them directly. However, a grandfather rule is necessary to achieve that objective with respect to existing investments, because some LAPTs have large shareholders and, under the documents under which the LAPTs are formed, the small investor would bear the economic burden of the withholding tax imposed because of the large holdings of others. Accordingly, this grandfather rule protects the LAPT investment in existing REIT shares. Future purchases of REIT shares by an LAPT must conform with the rules of sub-paragraph (4)(d) to be eligible for the 15 percent maximum rate.

www.ingramcontent.com/pod-product-compliance
Lightning Source LLC
Chambersburg PA
CBHW080631290526
45790CB00007B/3023